121287

HERITAGE OF BEAUTY

S. KRUCKENHAUSER

# HERITAGE OF BEAUTY

ARCHITECTURE AND SCULPTURE IN AUSTRIA

———

WITH AN INTRODUCTORY ESSAY

BY

E. H. GOMBRICH

LONDON

C. A. WATTS & CO. LTD

PRINTED IN AUSTRIA BY TIROLER GRAPHIK, INNSBRUCK

# CONTENTS

# INTRODUCTION

FOR those who know Austria Kruckenhauser's pictorial anthology should have a pleasant evocative power. Even though they may never have seen the majority of the individual sights he records with such loving care, his choice is so skilful that they will recall similar country churches, cloisters, roofs, courtyards or organ lofts teeming with music-making *putti*. His very method of grouping his motifs strengthens this impression of the typical. Following closely upon each other these images of porches or towers, of carvings or stucco are sufficiently varied not to look monotonous, and sufficiently alike to fuse and telescope in our minds merging, perhaps, with the memories of similar things we have seen on our own travels. For more often than not, what we recall from these travels is also distilled by our memory into typical configurations that may have lost their individual identity but retained a distinctive flavour. It takes an artist to catch this elusive feeling on the wing. The incomparable Osbert Lancaster with his flair for the authentic accents of a style, a type or a landscape has exploited this skill in his satires and travel books; so, in a different way, has Saul Steinberg. Unlike these draughtsmen the photographer is not free to vary the motif and retain only the characteristic, the frequent or the striking. His tools are selection, angles, lighting and juxtaposition. And yet the art historian may sometimes envy the power of these tools to bring out the character of a collective style. How much easier it is thus to present the essential physiognomy of late Gothic vaults or of Baroque cupolas than by a verbal analysis of their structural properties! How much more convincing are demonstrations of certain elusive continuities across the chronological limits of period styles than are our attempts to find a formula for regional traditions.

It is with such questions in mind, I submit, that we should approach Kruckenhauser's collection of photographs. For it goes without saying that the search for the typical must occasionally obscure the individual and the unique. Fragments of Michael Pacher's great St.-Wolfgang-Altar turn up like snatches of a melody in various places, but neither the whole altar nor its enchanting site is included. For this book is emphatically not intended as a tourist's guide to the principal beauties of Austria's landscape and art. For views of that country's most famous sights and monuments we must turn to the many excellent books of topographical illustrations that provide this information. What we find here is a subjective selection of more or less "hidden" treasures that struck the artist's eye. His programme excluded the styles of the nineteenth and twentieth century, it even cut out the whole art of painting as unsuitable for his medium. On the other hand it did not confine the roving artist strictly within the frontiers of present-day Austria, since at least three of his illustrations come from the South Tyrol that has belonged to Italy since 1919. But neither this lack of precision nor this extreme selectiveness disturbs the cumulative effect of this sequence as a composite picture of a country's artistic physiognomy.

True, Kruckenhauser's opening section transcends this question of local traditions, however closely it may be bound up with it. He illustrates the *building in its landscape setting* in a way that convinces us of the effortless harmony that seems to prevail between architecture and natural scenery in many an Alpine village. Not that this harmony is peculiar to the Alps. We all remember similar happy configurations from other old cities and villages of the Old and even the New World. No doubt our habits and subjective reactions have their share in this feeling of "rightness." Our nostalgia for the allegedly good old days and for the simple life envelops those sights in a deceptive haze that hides from us the tensions and the misfits of the past. The age and rarity of old buildings moreover renders them venerable even to the most hardened sceptic and will induce him to forget or forgive whatever may look arbitrary or badly solved in the joining of walls or placing of stairs. Few of us will ever arrive in front of an old castle or monastery in a frame of mind that favours criticism. We would no more wish the keep to be higher, the cupola to be steeper or the window to be lower than we would consciously wish the lines of the mountain to run differently. After a distance of time the past simply becomes part of nature, it merges with the scene. We feel so strongly that this type of building "belongs" in this kind of landscape that those could be forgiven who put down this reaction to simple conditioning. But is this all? The answer to this question is of much more than academic importance. It impinges on the urgent problem of the preservation of our heritage which is not only of relevance to the tourist trade. Have we no right to feel that this natural balance between landscape and architecture was once a reality and that it is really menaced by the modes of building that came in the wake of the industrial revolution, those standardized and mechanical "developments" that everywhere violate the beauty of the countryside? Will our garages and blocks of flats, our factories and our motels ultimately mellow and merge into the background as do the farm buildings and shrines on these pages? Will pylons look at least as innocuous as telegraph poles, cars as homely as oxcarts and television masts no more disturbing than the large clocks on the towers of village churches? One would like to hope so, but the chances are small. For there is at least one objective sense in which the old building can be said to merge into the landscape which can well be studied in these pages. Their variety in shape and in texture, the absence of regularity and uniformity softens the contrast between natural and man-made forms and facilitates that easy transition from trees to roofs, from peaks to towers that is so well brought out in some of the photographs. They confirm, I believe, the theories which were first worked out in eighteenth-century England by those critics who meditated on the nature of "Picturesque Beauty." It was a category invented to account for the requirements of the English garden — in contrast to the English country house built according to the severe laws of Palladian proportion. The villa is beautiful, the thatched cottage surrounded by creepers is picturesque, precisely because of the variety and irregularity of its appearance. Repetition and commercial exploitation have rendered the picturesque suspect. The thatched cottage within briars recalls the tea-cosy and "ye olde coffee shoppe." The functional architecture of the twentieth century glories in the hard-edged beauty of honest efficiency. It is only recently that the question has obtruded itself with increasing urgency on our architects and town planners whether the older methods and conditions of architecture that gave us the "picturesque" town, village or castle did not embody some other secret that eludes us? How can we recapture that feeling of "organic" unity with nature which a great modern architect such as Frank Lloyd Wright never ceased to demand, how can we escape the wasteland of "built-up areas" and give shape and meaning to our mushrooming towns? What makes for the superiority of traditional styles which was dimly felt and yet so badly traduced by the "historical" styles of the nineteenth century? Perhaps the answer may lie in the fact that these styles are indeed traditional and thus the result of a relatively slow process of evolution and adaptation. In such a process one might expect features which are felt to be obtruding or disturbing to be gradually eliminated from the builder's repertory. If one farmhouse was less successful and looked odd and alien in its surroundings, the next builder might unconsciously feel his way towards a better solution that avoids the mistakes of the first. This would be the conservative, the "Burkeian" case for the slow evolution of tools and styles in the settled life of relatively static societies, conditions that guarantee the successful adaptation to function and surroundings. Our aesthetic satisfaction with the results would thus be an intuitive acknowledgement of the "rightness" of these solutions within the requirements of a country's life and landscape. Nor would this "rightness" be restricted to utilitarian aspects. The steeple of the village church marking and accentuating the centre of the community's life and worship, the castle on the hill that slowly developed from a fortress into a commodious residence of the local Lord, the wealthy monastery set apart in its large estate, they all gradually find the form that suits both their function and their significance within the fabric of a country's life. This continuous significance, moreover, this sense of growth may transcend the changes of style and fashion that were bound to occur in the long history of a building. Few works of architecture were ever built precisely as they were envisaged on the drawing board. Few of the churches and castles illustrated in these pages did not undergo severe radical changes, additions and subtractions in the course of centuries; yet the Romanesque steeple seems to blend in with the Gothic nave, the Gothic vault with the Baroque organ almost as effortlessly as the whole seemed to blend with the landscape. Is our tolerance towards such incongruities of style yet another symptom of our sentimental indulgence or are stylistic hybrids more offensive to the doctrinaire than they are to the art lover? No doubt such clashes can jar. No doubt it happened quite often that a new generation despised and rejected the handiwork of their forebears and ignored or destroyed as much of it as was economically feasible. But there are other cases where we can prove that earlier phases of a building were respected and preserved and the new additions were made to fit in with the old. The most convincing examples of such tact and piety are the façade of St. Stephen's cathedral in Vienna (only partly visible on page 64) in which the Gothic extension was clearly designed to develop and echo the Romanesque core, and the Gothic vaults built by the Baroque architect Munggenast in Zwettl (page 162). But why should not others also have been responsive to this task of fitting the new to the old? Would a designer of a Baroque organ for a Gothic loft not quite instinctively have taken the shape of the church into account, however much his vocabulary of swags and scrolls may have differed from the tracery of the gallery (page 181)? Is not the story told that Meinrad Guggenbichler of Mondsee who carved the Baroque altars of St. Wolfgang (pages 202, 203) pleaded for the retention of Pacher's Gothic masterpiece on the high altar (pages 195, 223, 248, 251)? It was only the doctrinaire nineteenth century that invariably advocated a clean sweep and a restoration in the "pure Gothic style." The results, of course, were the worst unintentional hybrids of devotional art that crowded out so much that was genuine. If Austria's churches are still rich in the picturesque medleys of styles this is due to the fact that Austria was spared a Viollet le Duc and other learned gothicizers.

The typical Austrian village church combines a late Gothic structure with a late Baroque stucco decoration. This is not, perhaps, a mixture which will immediately appeal to English taste. For neither the late Gothic style of the fifteenth century that produced the complex vaults and the richly carved altars frequently displayed in the following pages nor the exuberant decorations of the Baroque with which our author is in love obey the canons of taste and restraint on which English critics have insisted throughout the eighteenth and nineteenth centuries. A glance through this book will show that for the Austrian craftsman richness and profusion, splendour and variety were never values to be shunned as was the case both in Italy and in the North during the predominance of the classical doctrine. The local builders and carvers were never inhibited by fear of being "vulgar" or "ornate." It is true that their idiom on the whole remained heavier and less capricious than the extreme styles of flamboyant Gothic in Spain or the wildest fancies of the Bavarian Rococo. But like the English Grinling Gibbons they loved the display of intricacy and ingenuity. Faced with the traditional sneer that their design resembled a wedding cake they might well have retorted — but what's wrong with a wedding cake?

But though the *Pocket Oxford Dictionary* of 1934 still gives as the first definition of the term *baroque* "grotesque, whimsical," the writings of Sacheverell Sitwell and the influx of art historians from Germany and Austria have softened the traditional English resistance against this Popish style of extravagance and over-statement. Maybe the time has come when an English tourist or reader can respond with a feeling of "rightness" to these rocking *putti* and billowing clouds. Austrians at any rate take these impressions as much for granted when they enter a church as they expect the scent of incense and the sound of eighteenth-century church music. Was it not Haydn who replied to the reproach that his Masses sounded too gay and worldly that he could not help this — the thought of heaven filled him with so much joy?

Coming down the Danube on his musical journey in 1772 Dr. Burney noticed that "all the way to Vienna the common people, in the public houses, and the labourers, at their work, divert themselves with singing in two or sometimes more parts ... almost all the young people that were walking by the waterside, were frequently singing, and never in less than two parts."

"It is not easy" (continues the doctor) "to account for this facility of singing in different parts, in the people of one country, more than in those of another: whether it arises in Roman Catholic countries, from the frequency of hearing music sung in parts, in their churches, I cannot say."

Dr. Burney's observation is relevant to this book only because it raises the question how a tradition is created and spreads, how certain habits of form and certain standards of skill penetrate far beyond the narrow sphere of the professional master active in a nation's capital, and how it imbues the whole life of a country. Polyphony was once a learned style that was indeed spread by the Church before it became the property of folk music. But this enjoyment of music in its turn provided the fertile soil from which sprang the flower of the Viennese classics.

To be sure, the situation in the visual arts is not quite the same, since fewer people can learn to carve than to sing. But if Kruckenhauser's book is intended to demonstrate anything it is the spread of certain forms and standards far beyond the main centres deep into the remotest valleys. Here, too, the impulses mainly came from the Church. The historian can often trace their origin into distant times and lands; in Austria he may be struck by two outstanding features he does not usually expect to find together — the timelag that often separates the country's artistic production from the prevailing styles of Western Europe and a profusion of local talent that guarantees high standards.

The strangely barbaric thirteenth-century sculpture of Schöngrabern (pages 216—19) is indeed a remote flowering of the Romanesque which had long been superseded in France by the beauty of

Gothic statuary. It is only in the fourteenth century that Austrian Gothic responds immediately to European developments originating from Italy, from Paris and from Prague. The fifteenth century finds Austria again hitched off from those dramatic changes that overcame the arts of Flanders and of Florence, though the South Tyrolean Michael Pacher was in contact with the art of Mantegna, and the master of Kefermarkt (pages 244—5) is a match to the craftsmen of Nuremberg. The Renaissance movement as such nearly passed Austria by, the great exception almost proving the rule — for the cenotaph that the Emperor Maximilian erected in Innsbruck (pages 198—9) harks back in its themes to the vanished glories of medieval chivalry. Even the wave of the Baroque that originated in Rome reached Austria relatively late, having passed through the modifying filter of Piedmontese variants and Lombard pattern books. For this new style was largely carried to Austria by migrant builders and decorators from Northern Italy who wandered north in the seventeenth and eighteenth centuries offering their services to princes and parishes who wanted their buildings modernized.

The role of these humble virtuosi is not perhaps sufficiently appreciated even now. Understandably official Austrian art history prefers to talk of Prandtauer the local man who built the glorious monastery of Melk rather than of Beduzzi the travelling "theatrical engineer" who supplied designs for its decorative details. Whatever their mutual share, it is clear that the indigenous craftsmen knew how to profit from the Italian invasion and how to absorb and revitalize the message that had thus reached them from distant Rome. The wealth of commissions that came to them in the wake of the Counter-reformation is reflected in these pages. Of course masters such as Fischer von Erlach and Hildebrand in Salzburg and Vienna were in touch with international developments, but the broad stream of the Austrian Baroque kept its impetus after the neo-classical reaction was well on the way in France and even in Rome. To be sure, artistic quality need never suffer because it is practised in a backwater. Even Bach's music was old-fashioned in its own time, and Tiepolo was something of an anachronism even in Italy. Yet in both these famous examples the special conditions under which these masters created gave them enough zest and confidence not to be overawed by changes in fashions elsewhere. The same, in a way, may be true of Austria's leading masters. For though they found themselves in a country near the fringe of Christendom they were yet near the centre of power — the family domain of Europe's dominant dynasty.

In no country of Europe is the feudal medieval past closer than it is in Austria. The writer of these lines still remembers the funeral of Francis Joseph in 1916, that sombre wartime pageantry marking the end of a reign that had started in 1848 with the suppression of the liberal revolution. One used to look with wonder and incredulity at the full title of the Emperor as it was printed on the title-page of the *Krippenkalender*, the Austrian equivalent of *Whitaker's Almanack*. For this title reflected a conception of sovereignty utterly different from that of a head of a state. The monarchy was no "state," it was an accumulation of domains and of partly fictitious claims that had been gathered up by the ruling family in the course of many centuries. The Emperor of Austria was also apostolic *King* of Hungary, of Bohemia, Dalmatia, Croatia, Slavonia, Lodomeria and Illyria — not to speak of the title of King of Jerusalem he still claimed. He was *Archduke* of Austria, *Grand Duke* of Tuscany (in name only), and of Cracow, *Duke* of Lorraine (by title), of Salzburg, Styria, Carinthia, Carniola and Bukowina, *Grand Prince* of Transylvania, *Margrave* of Moravia, *Duke* of Upper and Lower Silesia, of Modena, Parma, Piacenza and Guastalla (again without effective rights), of Auschwitz and Zator, Teschen, Friaul, Ragusa and Zara, *Count (of princely rank)* of Habsburg and Tyrol, of Kyburg, Gorizia and Gradisca, *Prince* of Trient and Brixen, *Margrave* of the high and the low Lausitz and in Istria,

*Count* of Hohenems, Feldkirch, Bregenz, Sonnenberg, etc., *Lord* of Trieste, Cattaro and the Windisch Mark, *Grand Voyvode* of Serbia, and so almost *ad infinitum*.

Only a full commentary of this motley list would provide a framework for the history of that region that was to become Austria. One point would rapidly emerge from such a history. If the Nazi crowds of 1938 greeted Hitler with the chant of *Heim ins Reich* (return home to the Reich) they were falsifying history through equivocation. The *Reich* or Empire of which the Austrian domains once formed a part was not of course the German *Reich* but the Holy Roman Empire, that strange fiction created by or for Charlemagne according to which the Roman Emperors had at last found a successor in the King of the Franks. This Empire, it will be remembered, was elective and subject to ratification by the Pope, and the history of central Europe during the subsequent centuries is largely the history of the intrigues and suffering this unrealistic institution involved. In the early Middle Ages the region around Vienna had become known as the *Ostmark*, the Eastern Marches, which developed into a prosperous duchy under the Babenberg dynasty, one of whose representatives is known to English history as the captor of Richard Lionheart who had to be ransomed from his prison in Dürnstein (1193). But Austria's destiny was really decided towards the end of the thirteenth century when the usual quarrels among the Electors resulted in the choice of a comparatively weak and landless Swiss Count, Rudolf of Habsburg. To assert his authority the newly elected King (he never had himself crowned Emperor) turned on the King of Bohemia who had been invested by Richard of Cornwall (a previous choice of the Electors) with the fiefs of the Babenbergs. Having defeated the Bohemian Rudolf bestowed the fief on his two sons (1282) and thus his dynasty became a power to be reckoned with.

Austria's subsequent history is the history of the Habsburg dynasty trying to enlarge and fortify these family domains and thus securing a base from which to enforce their election as Emperors. The accession of each of the Austrian lands is connected with another shake of the kaleidoscope of power. Marriages remaining without issue, heirs dying before coming of age, dynastic alliances, arbitrations and legal pretences all play their part in this immensely complex power game. The "will of the people" of course did not count any more in the Austrian lands than it did elsewhere in those feudal ages. If the nobility and the "Estates" proved recalcitrant they were crushed — and only the Swiss peasants who inhabited the Habsburgs' country of origin succeeded in eluding their grip. For like all medieval sovereigns the Habsburgs really looked at their lands as on their family estate; strangely enough they were very slow even in accepting the political advantage of *primogeniture*, the inheritance of the whole domains by the eldest son. Countless times the patchwork of properties was divided up between a ruler's heirs and without the high rate of infant mortality prevailing in those centuries the Habsburg power would soon have been dissipated by fragmentation and family feuds. As it was, the lands usually reverted again to the surviving line and though there were plenty of setbacks in the Habsburgs' bid for European power their estates kept extending.

Paradoxically perhaps it was during the first of these setbacks in the fourteenth century when the Imperial crown had gone to the Luxemburgs residing in Prague that one of the Habsburg dukes, Rudolf IV, made the most determined effort to raise the power, prosperity and prestige of his lands. By means of brazenly concocted "privileges" he demanded the unprecedented title of "archduke" for himself and his successors and thus staked a claim for the Habsburgs to stand higher in the pecking order than any other family. It was from these foundations that the house began its spectacular rise that is often summed up in the Latin tag: *bella gerant alii, tu felix Austria nube* (let others wage war, you, happy Austria, marry). For Albert, Duke of Austria, married the daughter of the Emperor

Sigismund and thus come to unite in his person the crowns of Bohemia and of Hungary. He died in 1439 soon after his election but Frederick the Habsburg Duke of Styria now took over the inheritance and soon also the Imperial dignity. Though both the Bohemian and the Hungarian crowns eluded him, though he even temporarily lost Vienna first to his brother and then to the Hungarians, this notoriously inept monarch transformed the situation of his house by marrying his son Maximilian to the daughter of the Duke of Burgundy in 1477. Their son Philip married Joan of Castille, the heiress to the Spanish dominions, in 1496 and so Maximilian's grandson Charles V (who also inherited the Austrian possessions in 1519) stood at the pinnacle of power at the very time when the Spanish *conquistadores* seized parts of the New World; whence his often quoted boast that the sun never set in his domains. Geographically that was not far from the truth, but the reign of Charles V also witnessed the emergence of three distinctive threats to the tranquillity of Habsburg land-collecting — the success of the Reformation which undermined the religious foundations of the Holy Roman Empire, the menace from the Turks who crushed Hungary and advanced as far as Vienna (1529), and the shift of sea power towards the Atlantic seaboard that followed on the age of discovery. This is not the place, of course, to recite the crises and sufferings that ensued for the Austrian lands during the religious wars of the seventeenth century. Protestantism had made many converts among the population and even among the nobility and the means by which these recalcitrant subjects were coerced back into the fold of the Church or expelled the country do not make pleasant reading. An Austrian bully will still use the menacing expression: "I'll make you a Catholic yet."

Moreover the ascendancy of the Spanish line over the Austrian cousins gradually led to the dominance of Spanish etiquette in the Vienna court with its international Catholic culture. The political turning point came when the Turks failed in their second siege of Vienna in 1683 and the Austrian armies under Prince Eugene of Savoy embarked on a war of liberation that extended the frontiers of the Habsburg domain as far as Transylvania. It was in these years of buoyancy during the first decades of the eighteenth century with the victory of the Catholic camp assured at home and abroad, that the Baroque style established itself in the Austrian landscape. The extinction of the male line after the death of Charles VI in 1740 led to a fresh crisis when Frederick of Prussia challenged the succession of Maria Theresa. Yet the pretence of the Holy Roman Empire continued till Napoleon's assumption of the Imperial title in 1804 led Francis of Habsburg to assume the title of Emperor of Austria. The humiliations which the Habsburgs suffered under Napoleon still led to one happy result — in the general rearrangement of the map  the independent Archbishopric of Salzburg, that jewel of a city, was joined to Austria.

Who, except professional historians still remembers these dates and deals? What is remembered is the emergence of Vienna as one of Europe's cultural centres, however much a Metternich might try to seal it off against the dangerous influences of foreign ideas. He could not prevent the contagion of nationalism that erupted in 1848 and first led to the loss of most of the Monarchy's North Italian possessions. Yet, by a succession of compromises and balancing acts the Habsburgs maintained themselves on the top of that unstable pyramid while the industrial revolution and universal education brought the explosive issue of languages in the polyglot monarchy increasingly to the fore. Defeat in the first world war and the idea of "self-determination" completed the disintegration of the ancient feudal edifice and brought the German-speaking subjects of the Empire face to face with the question of their own identity. Their conflicting answers to this question are writ large across the tragic history of the last thirty years. It looks as if their forcible incorporation in Hitler's *Reich* had convinced many Austrians of the continued relevance of their different past.

This need not imply that they must take refuge in nostalgia for splendours that were often dearly bought. Indeed, it is understandable that many Austrians prefer to remind the world of the achievement of Vienna's socialists in their welfare work or of the world fame of such men as Freud, Mahler, Schönberg or Kokoschka. The Vienna Circle in philosophy, the Vienna schools of economics, of medicine and even of the history of art have played a part in this century that justifies the Austrians' distaste of the advertiser's clichés. No citizen of any country will take kindly to the commercialized simplifications for simpletons that the tourist industry seems to need. England is not a country of fox hunters and beef eaters, nor is Italy an art gallery with an *osteria* attached to it. Austria is neither a country of yodelling yokels nor of waltzing aristocrats. But in Kruckenhauser's pictures something is caught of the real old Austria which an Austrian can accept as authentic.

E. H. GOMBRICH

# A TECHNICAL NOTE

HERR Kruckenhauser, whose early book *Snow Canvas* was published in English in 1937 derives the peculiarities of his photographic technique from the films in praise of skiing which made history in the middle twenties. It was from Fanck's film *Wunder des Schneeschuhs* that he learned to appreciate the artistic potentialities of the tele-objective. With a great focal length the distortions of wide-angle photographs are avoided. To achieve similar focal lengths with large plate cameras clumsy and heavy equipment is needed that cannot be carried in a rucksack. It was this consideration that led Herr Kruckenhauser to the Leica. A Universal Viewfinder helps him to establish the required focal length and to select the appropriate lens (Elmar 10.5 cm, Hektor 13.5 cm, Telyt 20 and 40 cm). To compensate for the needs of enlargement slow fine-grade films were used. More than eighty per cent of the pictures in this book were taken in this way. Herr Kruckenhauser's favourite technique and medium dictated his selection of motifs. It enabled him to pick out the significant detail in telling close-ups of architecture and sculpture and to avoid excessive distortion when tilting the camera upwards. His aim, of course, was not the conventional picture postcard nor the informative surveyor's photograph but the revelation of aspects that eludes their methods. Both the arrangement of these motifs and their juxtaposition in the double spreads serve this end.

1

FLIESS
TIROL

MÜNICH
TIROL

FISS
TIROL

NAUDERS
TIROL

TERNDORF
SALZBURG

8

FORCHTENSTE
BURGENLAND

ST. LEONHARD
OB.-ÖSTERR.

SCHLAINING
BURGENLAND

7

MELK
ED.-ÖSTERR.

SENFTENBERG
NIED.-ÖSTERR.

HIRSCHBACH
OB.-ÖSTERR.

LILIENFELD
NIED.-ÖSTERR.

RETZ
NIED.-ÖSTERR.

ZUG
VORARLBERG

ST. LORENZEN
NIED.-ÖSTERR.

STUBEN
VORARLBERG

ARTHOLOMÄBERG
VORARLBERG

HALLSTATT
OB.-ÖSTERR.

GEMAIS
TIROL

LANERSBACH
TIROL

HOLLERSBACH
SALZBURG

HEILIGENBLUT
KÄRNTEN

MONDSEE
OB.-ÖSTERR.

OBERWANG
OB.-ÖSTERR.

ARZL
TIROL

PULKAU
NIED.-ÖSTERR.

ST. LEONHARD
SALZBURG

2

MALS
SÜDTIROL

FRIEDERSBACH
NIED.-ÖSTERR.

ALM
SALZBURG

HALLSTATT
OB.-ÖSTERR.

VOLDERS
TIROL

AURACH
TIROL

LECH
VORARLBERG

LEIBLFING
TIROL

KITZBÜHEL
TIROL

ST. LORENZ
OB.-ÖSTERR.

GURK
KÄRNTEN

MARIA SAAL
KÄRNTEN

INNSBRUCK
TIROL

MARIENBERG
SÜDTIROL

ST. STEFAN
WIEN

ST. STEFAN
WIEN

ST. STEFAN
WIEN

MARIA
AM GESTADE
WIEN

MARIA
STRASSENGEL
STEIERMARK

BRAUNAU
OB.-ÖSTERR.

SALZBURG

ZWETTL
NIED.-ÖSTERR.

KARLSKIRCHE
WIEN

PÖLLAU
STEIERMA

MELK
ND.-ÖSTERR.

SALZBURG

SALZBURG

FISS
TIROL

3

HÄGERAU
TIROL

KRISTBERG
VORARLBERG

TUX
TIROL

ST. MICHAE
NIED.-ÖSTE

DÜRNSTEIN
NIED.-ÖSTERR.

LILIENFELD
NIED.-ÖSTER

STEIN
-ÖSTERR.

AMRAS
TIROL

SCHLAINING
BURGENLAND

GRAZ
STEIERMARK

GRAZ
STEIERMARK

BURG

SALZBURG

SALZBURG

SALZBURG

4

TEMPLUM
HONORIBUS
B.MARIÆ.V
ASSUMTÆ
DICATUM

LILIENFELD
NIED.-ÖSTERR.

SALZBURG

GRAZ
STEIERMARK

DÜRNSTEIN
NIED. ÖSTERR.

RETZ
NIED.-ÖSTERR.

THOMAS VERDERBERS NEFFEN

THOMAS VERDERBERS NEFFEN

MELK
NIED.-ÖSTERR.

SALZBURG

BRUCK
STEIERMARK

1

EISENSTADT
BURGENLAND

SALZBURG

ALZBURG

SPITTAL
KÄRNTEN

ST. FLORIAN
OB.-ÖSTERR.

ST. FLORIAN
OB.-ÖSTERR.

ST. FLORIAN
OB.-ÖSTERR.

ST. STEFAN
WIEN

STEFAN
WIEN

SCHÖNGRABERN
NIED.-ÖSTERR.

GURK
KÄRNTEN

WIEN

1

SALZBURG

IN CONCEPTIONE
IMMACULATA PERMANSISTI
ET NOBIS CHRISTUM
PEPERISTI.

SALZBURG

WIEN

INNSBRUCK
TIROL

5

ZWETTL
NIED.-ÖSTERR.

ZWETTL
NIED.-ÖSTERR.

ST. STEFAN
WIEN

ST. STEFAN
WIEN

ST. VALENTIN
NIED.-ÖSTERR.

SCHWAZ
TIROL

MARIA SAAL
KÄRNTEN

MARIA SAAL
KÄRNTEN

WIENER
NEUSTADT
NIED.-ÖSTERR.

GURK
KÄRNTEN

1

GURK
KÄRNTEN

LILIENFELD
NIED.-ÖSTERR.

ST. PAUL
KÄRNTEN

HEILIGENK
NIED.-ÖSTE

HEILIGENKREUZ
NIED.-ÖSTERR.

EISENSTADT
BURGENLAND

LILIENFELD
D.-ÖSTERR.

INNSBRUC[K]
TIROL

FLORIAN
-ÖSTERR.

SPITTAL
KÄRNTEN

ST. FLORIAN
OB.-ÖSTERR.

ST. FLORIAN
OB.-ÖSTERR.

ST. FLORIAN
OB.-ÖSTERR.

ST. FLORIAN
OB.-ÖSTERR.

1

6

GURK
KÄRNTEN

GRAZ
STEIERMARK

GURK
KÄRNTEN

ZWETTL
ÖSTERR.

ZWETTL
NIED.-ÖSTE

ZWETTL
N.-ÖSTERR.

ST. PAUL
KÄRNTEN

ST. PAUL
KÄRNTEN

ST. PAUL
KÄRNTEN

GÖSS
STEIERMARK

1

GURK
KÄRNTEN

1

MELK
NIED.-ÖSTE

1

MARIA SAAL
KÄRNTEN

HERZOGENBU
NIED.-ÖSTER

STAMS
TIROL

SPECIES · TIBI · CVM · PACE · DATVR ·

MELK
NIED.-ÖSTE.

VORAU
STEIERMA

7

MARIA GAIL
KÄRNTEN

LIEDING
KÄRNTEN

CHRISTKINDL
OB.-ÖSTERR.

ST. WOLFGA
OB.-ÖSTERR.

ST. WOLFGANG
OB.-ÖSTERR.

MONDSEE
OB.-ÖSTERR.

ST. WOLFGANG
OB.-ÖSTERR.

ST. WOLFGANG
OB.-ÖSTERR.

SALZBURG

JUDENBURG
STEIERMARK

8

9

MARIA
STRASSENGEL
STEIERMARK

MAUER
NIED.-ÖSTERR.

224

ST. WOLFGANG
OB.-ÖSTERR.

23

SALZBURG

ST. VEIT
KÄRNTEN

MAUER
NIED.-ÖSTERR.

MAUER
NIED.-ÖSTERR.

MAUER
NIED.-ÖST

MONDSEE
OB.-ÖSTERR.

IRRSDORF
SALZBURG

WIENER
NEUSTADT
NIED.-ÖSTERR.

INZERSDORF
OB.-ÖSTERR.

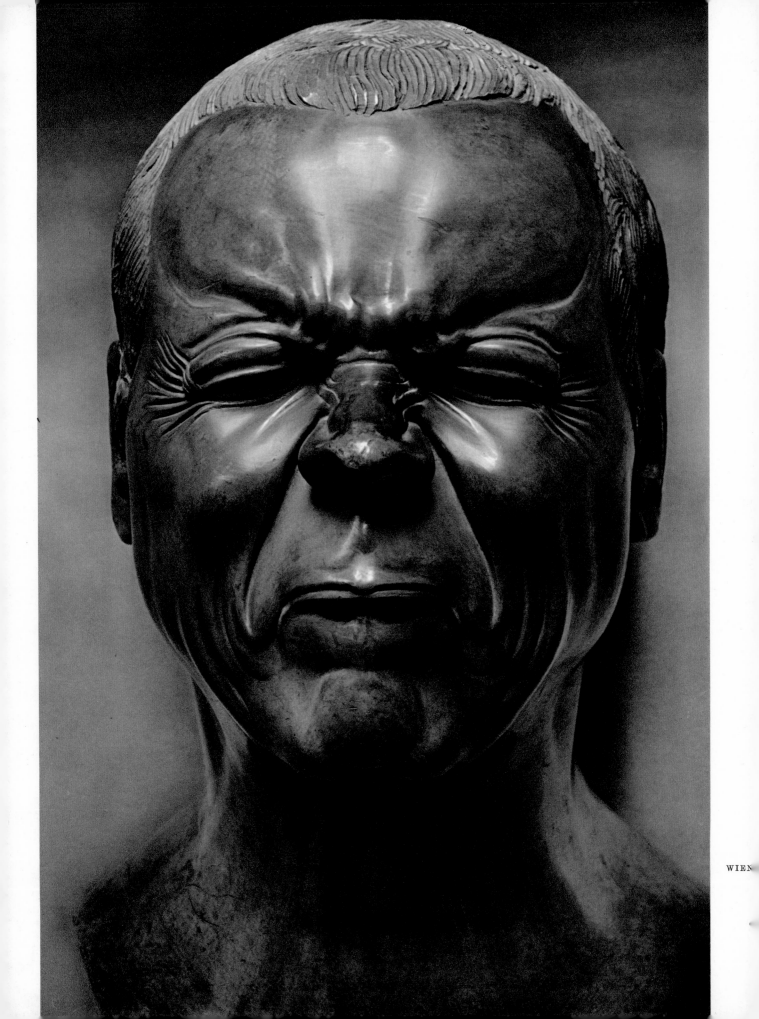

WIENER
NEUSTADT
NIED.-ÖST

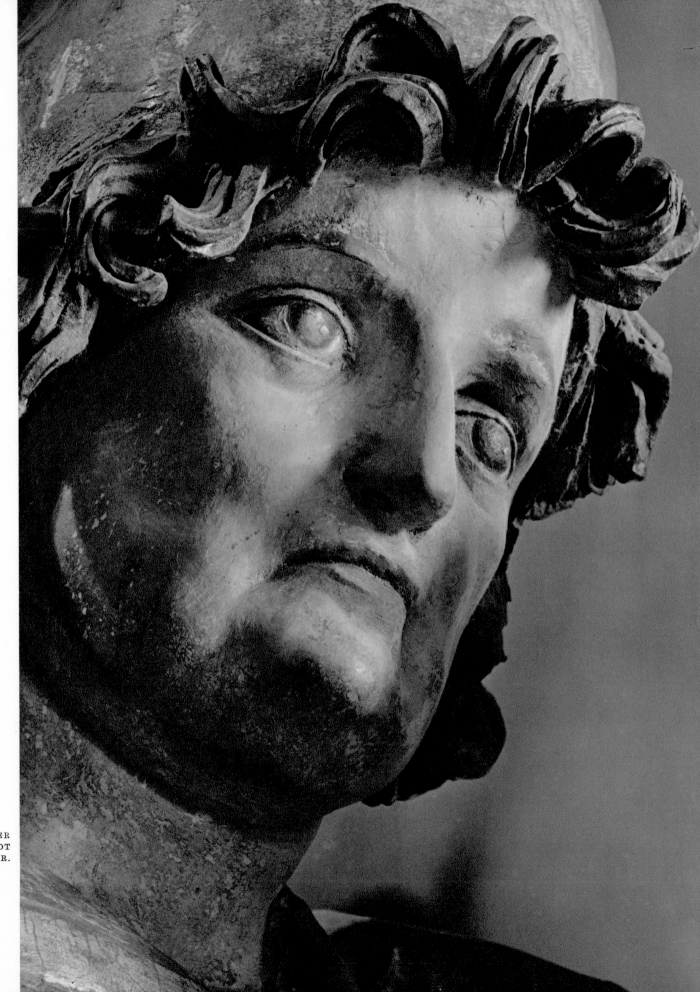

MONDSEE
OB.-ÖSTERR.

IRRSDORF
SALZBURG

KEFERMA
OB.-ÖSTE

IRRSDORF
SALZBURG

NOTES ON THE ILLUSTRATIONS

18: FLIESS, TYROL. The new parish church was built between 1794 and 1804 in a neo-classicist idiom. The twin towers are crowned by the characteristic bulbous spires of the Baroque period.

19: KRAKAUEBENE, STYRIA. A large farmstead, called a *Zwiehof* consisting of two large buildings, one the dwelling house, the other comprising the stables, barn and granary. This type of building is frequently found in the hilly regions of Austria.

20: REITH NEAR KITZBÜHEL, TYROL. Münichau, a picturesque castle, probably first built in the mid fifteenth century was gutted by fire in 1914. It was rebuilt, and recently enlarged to become a luxury hotel and was opened as such in 1964.

21: FISS, TYROL. The church tower has large Gothic windows and a bulbous spire dating from 1717 that rises above the small village.

22: NAUDERS, TYROL. The stone-built houses of this mountain village with their timbered attics and wooden-tiled roofs are set closely together.

23: MAUTERNDORF, SALZBURG. The church of St. Gertrude surrounded by a cemetery lies outside the village. The building dates from the twelfth century, but there was considerable rebuilding subsequently and additions were made later including the bulbous spire which was added in the eighteenth century and the whole church was restored in 1926. It contains fine altars and remarkable decorations.

24: FORCHTENSTEIN, BURGENLAND. The castle which dates from the thirteenth century has belonged to the Esterhazy family since 1622. In the seventeenth century many additions were made both to the fortifications and to the residential quarters.

25: SCHLAINING, BURGENLAND. The medieval castle and its impressive tower date from the thirteenth century and have survived unaltered. Alterations were made, however, to the fortifications during the seventeenth century to enable them to withstand the new methods of warfare. *See* 27, 91.

26: ST. LEONHARD, UPPER AUSTRIA. A village of large stone-built farmhouses with thatched roofs. The four wings of a farmhouse are arranged round a square courtyard (*Vierkanthof*) a form that is characteristic of the large farmsteads of Upper Austria.

27: SCHLAINING, BURGENLAND. Another view of the castle, showing the later additions to the building. *See* 25, 91.

28: LUBEREGG, LOWER AUSTRIA. A castle, opposite Melk, overlooking the Danube. It is Baroque in style although built in 1780; the centre pavilion with a hipped roof rises above the wings.

29: MELK ON THE DANUBE, LOWER AUSTRIA. The Benedictine monastery and its church are situated high above the Danube, and command a wide view of the landscape. The present building which was built between 1702 and 1736 was designed by Jakob Prandtauer, a great architect of monastic buildings in Austria. *See* 75, 108, 176, 184.

30: SENFTENBERG NEAR KREMS ON THE DANUBE, LOWER AUSTRIA. The fortified church is situated on a mountain slope outside the village. Built in the early sixteenth century its form is late Gothic; the interior was remodelled in the eighteenth century

31: HIRSCHBACH, UPPER AUSTRIA. The late Gothic church dates from the end of the fifteenth century. Extensive restoration has destroyed much of its original character.

32: LILIENFELD, LOWER AUSTRIA. The Cistercian abbey was founded in 1202 and its church dedicated in 1230. The apse, the square ambulatory — a very rare feature — and the high transept were probably finished by that time; the nave (the ridge of the roof can be seen) is slightly later in date, and the tower was rebuilt after a fire in 1810. *See* 88, 102, 144, 149.

33: RETZ, LOWER AUSTRIA. A view of the town which was founded towards the end of the thirteenth century. The most outstanding feature is the town hall with its massive Gothic tower crowned by a Baroque onion cupola-cum-spire; to the right of it one can catch a glimpse of a house on the market square. In the left foreground the Dominican abbey and church can be seen and behind it the Baroque tower of yet another church. *See* 107.

34: ZUG NEAR LECH, VORARLBERG. Small village church surrounded by timbered houses with their characteristic low roofs.

35: ST. LORENZEN, LOWER AUSTRIA. The Gothic village church rebuilt in 1409 with a massive tower and a square chancel stands on the shores of the Danube. This type of church with the short stone spire is characteristic of the region.

36: STUBEN, VORARLBERG. The parish church was built early in the sixteenth century; the tower was rebuilt in the eighteenth century and crowned with the large bulbous cupola.

37: BARTHOLOMÄBERG, VORARLBERG. Roof of a farmhouse. Horizontal rafters are laid over the wooden tiles and weighted down by stones to withstand Alpine storms.

38: HALLSTATT, UPPER AUSTRIA. The very curious wooden spire rising in four stages above the stone tower of the Roman Catholic parish church, dates from the second half of the eighteenth century. It is somehow reminiscent of Norwegian spires. *See 250.*

39: LANERSBACH, TYROL. Timbered huts high up in the Alps; the very low roofs are weighted down by stones. *See 41.*

40: GEMAIS, TYROL. These farmhouses, some quite large, are constructed entirely of timber. Various building techniques are employed. Strong wooden fences at the sides of the road prevent cattle from straying.

41: LANERSBACH, TYROL. Wooden huts, roofed with characteristic wooden tiles weighted down with stones. These huts, built high up in the Alps serve as summer quarters for cowherds and dairymaids.

42: HOLLERSBACH, SALZBURG. The farmhouses are built of timber on a stone foundation. Their outbuildings and the fences surrounding them are constructed entirely of timber.

43: HEILIGENBLUT, CARINTHIA. A large farmhouse outside the village: it is built entirely of timber and roofed with wooden shingles.

44: OBERWANG, UPPER AUSTRIA. St. Konrad built in 1450 and restored in 1745 stands in a lonely position outside a village.

45: MONDSEE, UPPER AUSTRIA. A little wayside chapel with an overhanging roof, open at the front; it shelters a crucifixion group.

46: ARZL, TYROL. The Stations of the Cross lead up to the polygonal church with a large dome; the single tower is crowned with a bulbous cupola. The church, built in 1666 and restored in 1777, stands on the brow of a hill offering a wide view to the pilgrim.

47: PULKAU, LOWER AUSTRIA. The parish church lies outside the village on a slight hill of this rolling countryside. The pointed roof next to the church is that of the *Karner*, or charnel house, a building characteristic of this region, in which the bones from disused tombs were collected.

48: ST. LEONHARD, SALZBURG. This fortified Gothic church with a very pointed spire on the north side — a companion tower had possibly been planned for the South side — was built by Peter Harperger of Salzburg between the years 1430 and 1433.

## 2 TOWERS AND CUPOLAS

50: MALS, SOUTH TYROL. The church of St. Benedict dates from the ninth century, and the massive Romanesque towers with their squat roofs from the thirteenth century. The church, a rare example of Carolingian architecture, is now no longer used for worship.

51: FRIEDERSBACH, LOWER AUSTRIA. The parish church begun in Romanesque style in the twelfth century was rebuilt in Gothic style in the fifteenth century. The *Karner* in front which is the usual round shape with a high conical roof dates from the fourteenth century.

52: ALM, SALZBURG. The parish church which is also a place of pilgrimage, was dedicated in 1506. The spire, particularly high and pointed seems to try to compete with the high mountain behind it.

53: HALLSTATT, UPPER AUSTRIA. The Protestant church was built in 1862 in the Gothic Revival style.

54: VOLDERS, TYROL. The church dedicated to St. Charles Borromaeus lies just outside Innsbruck. It is one of the rare early-seventeenth-century Baroque churches in Austria,

designed by Hippolyt Guarinoni. Building was begun in 1620 and completed in 1654. The richly decorated tower is crowned with a somewhat squashed bulbous cupola.

55: AURACH, TYROL. The church was dedicated in 1427. The Gothic tower has a large and particularly wide bulbous cupola.

56: LECH, VORARLBERG. The massive fourteenth-century tower is crowned with a very large onion cupola which dwarfs the church.

57: LEIBLFING, TYROL. The parish church with its mighty tower was built towards the end of the fifteenth century. The bulbous cupola-cum-spire together with the top storey was added in 1710.

58: KITZBÜHEL, TYROL. Of the two adjoining churches, one is the parish church of St. Andrew, begun in 1435, dedicated in 1506 and partly refurbished in the Baroque manner in the eighteenth century (when the slender tower was given its Baroque finish) and thoroughly restored in the nineteenth and twentieth centuries. The *Liebfrauenkirche*, dedicated to the Virgin, dates from the fourteenth century and was built on to an even older massive tower.

59: ST. LORENZ, UPPER AUSTRIA. This church near Mondsee was dedicated in 1732. It has twin towers each one crowned with a bulbous spire balancing on the top of a four-cornered roof. The church has a flattish hipped roof.

60: GURK, CARINTHIA. The cathedral of Gurk is a major architectural work in the Romanesque style in Austria. It was completed about 1200; between 1679 and 1682 the western twin towers were given their bulbous spires. *See* 125, 142, 143, 158, 161, 172.

61: MARIA SAAL, CARINTHIA. A fortified late Gothic church built in the first half of the fifteenth century. The powerful west towers, somewhat different in character from the much earlier ones of Gurk cathedral, were given Baroque hoods after a fire in 1670. *See* 138, 139, 167, 179, 191, 192.

62: INNSBRUCK, TYROL. The clock tower (the *Stadtturm*) was first built in the fourteenth century. The double cupola and the four corner turrets were added in 1560 to 1561. The clock dates from 1602, and the sundial from the sixteenth century. The top of the mighty central feature is reminiscent of representations of the Holy Sepulchre on ivories or in illuminations of medieval manuscripts.

63: BURGUSIO (BURGEIS), SOUTH TYROL. The Benedictine Abbey Monte Maria (Marienberg) and its church have a history of much rebuilding. The original medieval buildings were erected in the twelfth century. The edifice was rebuilt in the seventeenth century and restored again in the nineteenth century. The single tower is crowned by a two-tiered onion cupola.

64: ST. STEPHEN'S, VIENNA. The so-called *Heidentürme*, the west towers of the original, smaller Romanesque building, were later given their Gothic spires; the steep roof which partly engulfs them belongs to the Gothic phase, during which the west façade was widened. See 65, 66, 122, 123, 134, 135, 166.

65: ST. STEPHEN'S, VIENNA. The tower and spire on the south side was completed in 1433; its companion to the north remained unfinished, probably for aesthetic rather than practical reasons. To the left the large steep roof, built in the mid fifteenth century is covered with coloured tiles; at the left of the photograph part of one of the two west towers can be seen and behind the tower the choir which dates from 1340 is visible. *See* 64, 66, 122, 123, 134, 135, 166.

66: ST. STEPHEN'S, VIENNA. The tower and spire of Vienna cathedral, the landmark of the town. See 64, 65, 122, 123, 134, 135, 166.

67: MARIA AM GESTADE, VIENNA. The tower with its traceried ogee hood — reminiscent of King's College Chapel Cambridge — was finished in 1350 and restored 1534—7. Like the tower of St. Stephen's it is on the south side of the church, where the choir joins the nave.

68: MARIA STRASSENGEL, STYRIA. The single octagonal tower with its tall traceried spire, is the outstanding feature of the pilgrimage church of St. Maria Strassengel. Church and tower were both built between the years 1346 and 1366. *See* 221.

69: BRAUNAU, UPPER AUSTRIA. This very elaborate late Gothic tower of this parish church was built in 1492; the top storey with the clock faces and the bulbous Baroque spire were added in 1759. *See* 174.

70: SALZBURG. A view of some of the many towers and domes of the city. Left is the church of St. Peter, originally a medieval church, rebuilt in the seventeenth and eighteenth centuries in the Baroque style; the bulbous spire and the dome resting on a high drum were finished in 1757. In the background is the dome of one of Fischer von Erlach's churches the *Kollegienkirche*. Of the two spires on the right, the little turret belongs to the St. Margaret's Chapel and the very elaborate Gothic tower with a Gothic Revival spire to the Franciscan church.

71: ZWETTL, LOWER AUSTRIA. The west front of the Church of the Cistercian Abbey designed by Matthias Steinde, was built by Josef Munggenast in the years 1722 to 1727. The richly decorated façade with its strongly accentuated axis merges nearly imperceptibly into the single tower crowned with a cupola. *See* 132, 133, 162—5.

72: VIENNA. The elliptical dome of the church of St. Charles Borromaeus seen from the back. The dome rests on an elaborately articulated drum and is finished with an ornate lantern. The little lantern on the right belongs to one of the giant columns which stand in front of the church. The *Karlskirche* built by J. B. Fischer von Erlach, was begun and finished in 1716—37.

73: SALZBURG. Another view of the spires and domes of Salzburg. On the right the bulbous spire of St. Peter's which dates from 1757 is seen. Next to it the dome of the cathedral and one of its west towers. Both these features are less ornate and more classical than their neighbour. The cathedral, the first Baroque church to be erected in Austria or Germany, was built between the years 1614 and 1628 after designs by the Italian architect Santino Solari.

74: PÖLLAU, STYRIA. This former abbey church, now the parish church was probably built between 1700 and 1710 by Joachim Carlone and Remigius Horner. It is a cool and restrained building in contrast to the many ornate Baroque churches.

75: MELK, LOWER AUSTRIA. The dome over the cross of the Abbey church was erected between 1712 and 1714 by Jakob Prandtauer. The dome rises in two stages, rather like a hipped roof, above a simply decorated drum, and is crowned with an elaborately decorated lantern. *See* 29, 108, 176, 184.

76 and 77: SALZBURG. The church of St. Erhard in Nonntal, outside Salzburg, has a central dome. It was built by Caspar Zugalli, begun in 1685 and finished in 1689.

78: FISS, TYROL. The Baroque hood, built *c.* 1717, of the Gothic tower rises high above the low roofs of the mountain village.

# 3 ROOFS

80: HÄGERAU, TYROL. View of the village, with its houses strung out along a road. The houses are very similar to each other, built partly of masonry or brick and partly of timber; they have flat roofs covered with wooden shingles weighted down by rafters and stones.

81: KRIMML, SALZBURG. The village which is built on a slope consists of large houses with the same type of roof as those in the Tyrol.

82: KRISTBERG, VORARLBERG. The houses and storage huts are built mainly of timber; the fairly flat roofs are covered with shingles and nailed to the roof timbers below.

83: TUX, TYROL. Alpine huts, constructed of horizontally arranged logs, a very ancient method of building. The roofs are constructed in the same way as those elsewhere in the Tyrol.

84: ST. MICHAEL, LOWER AUSTRIA. The apse, chancel, and part of the high nave of a fortified late Gothic church which was built between 1500 and 1523. In the foreground the houses of the village, which lies on the bank of the Danube, are seen set closely together.

85: TRAUNKIRCHEN, UPPER AUSTRIA. The parish church picturesquely situated on the shores of the lake was built as the church of a Jesuit monastery between 1631 and 1652. It is interesting because of its very varied roof formations; the polygonal apse which is now covered with a hipped roof copied from that of the west tower, was until 1804 also crowned with a tower.

86: DÜRNSTEIN, LOWER AUSTRIA. The closely built town is seen in the foreground; in the background is the former abbey of Augustinian Canons with its monastic building and its church close to the banks of the Danube. The Baroque tower, richly decorated was built between 1710 and 1740 almost certainly after designs of Jakob Prandtauer. *See* 87, 106.

87: DÜRNSTEIN, LOWER AUSTRIA. A view of another part of the little town showing the castle built in an early Baroque style in 1622; its four wings are arranged round a small square interior court. *See* 86, 106.

88: LILIENFELD, LOWER AUSTRIA. Another view of the Abbey of Lilienfeld. The Cistercian abbey was founded in 1202 and has been rebuilt several times. Extensive rebuilding took place in the seventeenth century. The edifice was restored for the last time after a disastrous fire in 1810. The west tower dates from this period. *See* 32, 102, 144, 149.

89: STEIN ON THE DANUBE, LOWER AUSTRIA. Former church of the Friars Minor *(Minoritenkirche)*. The lofty Gothic choir, characteristic of the buildings belonging to the Mendicant Orders was added in 1300 to the late Romanesque basilica of 1264. The bulbous spire dates from the eighteenth century.

90: CASTLE AMBRAS, TYROL. The granary of the castle is seen in the foreground, in the background is the castle itself which was rebuilt, 1564—7, in the style of the German Renaissance. The castle still houses remnants of the *Ambraser Sammlung*, a collection of works of art, which also formed the basis of the *Kunsthistorisches Museum* in Vienna.

91: SCHLAINING, BURGENLAND. The castle is in the background. The little town was founded in 1462. The layout of its streets is rather irregular and there is considerable variety in the size and design of its houses. *See* 25, 27.

92: GRAZ, STYRIA. A view of the roofs of the oldest part of the city. In the background is the mighty Baroque Palace of the Counts of Attems built *c.* 1702—16 by an architect of Italian extraction, Joachim Carlone. *See* 93—5.

93: GRAZ, STYRIA. A view from the *Schloßberg*, a formerly fortified hill in the centre of the town, of one of the many narrow courtyards and of the steep roofs of the houses in the oldest part of Graz. *See* 92, 94, 95.

94: GRAZ, STYRIA. In the foreground is an arcaded courtyard. It is typical of many houses, and gives them an Italian appearance. *See* 92, 93, 95.

95: GRAZ, STYRIA. The houses in this view from the *Schloßberg* are so closely set together, many of them are back to back, that one wonders where there is room for streets. Windows are placed wherever there is space for them. *See* 92, 93, 94.

96: STEYR, UPPER AUSTRIA. This view was taken from the tower of the parish church looking toward the river Steyr and shows the fairly regular rows of houses obviously built on plots of identical size.

97: SALZBURG. Roofs of the curious shape shown in this photograph are traditional in Salzburg and many were built as long ago as the Middle Ages. In the background is the famous *Kapitelschwemme*, one of several horse ponds that date from the Baroque period. *See* 98.

98: SALZBURG. The cathedral is seen in the background and in the foreground are more of Salzburg's curious roofs. *See* 73, 97.

99: SALZBURG. In the foreground is a monastery — the *Kajetanerkloster* built between 1685 and 1700 by Caspar Zugalli. In the background is the Nonnberg convent, the oldest nunnery of the Benedictines. The squashed-onion-shaped hood of the tower of the church, seen behind the convent, parts of which date from the twelfth century, was added in 1711.

100: SALZBURG. The University church, one of Fischer von Erlach's most famous buildings erected between 1694 and 1707. It is likely that the architect was in England in 1700: the design of the rounded façade together with its pediment is too like the apse of St. Paul's to be accidental. *See* 177.

# 4 DOORWAYS, COURTYARDS AND FAÇADES

102: LILIENFELD, LOWER AUSTRIA. The west porch of the abbey church dates from the mid thirteenth century; according to Cistercian rules it had to be without any decoration, yet the repetition of the shafts of the jambs and archivolts creates a powerful pattern. *See* 32, 144, 149.

103: GRAZ, STYRIA. The main portal of the *Leechkirche*, 1275—93. The Virgin and Child in the tympanum of the same period is an outstanding example of Austrian Early Gothic sculpture. The archivolts, because of their elaborate profiles, allow an interesting play of light and shade. *See* 213.

104: SALZBURG. A view of the *Residenzbrunnen*, 1656—61, and of the *Residenz*, the palace of the Archbishops of Salzburg erected between 1592 and 1602. *See* 114, 117, 159.

105: GRAZ, STYRIA. The arcaded quadrangle of the *Landhaus* the seat of the provincial government: a large building with several courtyards, it was begun in the sixteenth century, and finished in the nineteenth.

106: DÜRNSTEIN ON THE DANUBE, LOWER AUSTRIA. This entrance portal, the principal feature of the quadrangle of the famous abbey, was probably built to designs by Matthias Steindl. In arrangement it is similar to a Baroque altar-piece, and sculpture and architecture are so closely welded together that it is difficult to separate them. *See* 86, 87.

107: RETZ, LOWER AUSTRIA. This "column," a mixture of sculpture, architectural features, ornaments and clouds soaring upwards and representing the Trinity, is characteristic of many *Dreifaltigkeitssäulen* and similar *Pestsäulen*, erected to celebrate deliverance from the plague which frequently occurred in Austrian towns. This one shows a firmer architectural framework than most others; it dates from 1744. In the background is a mighty sixteenth-century house with crenellations, which can also be seen on page 33.

108: MELK ON THE DANUBE, LOWER AUSTRIA. The richly decorated principal entrance to the abbey was built 1723—4 from designs by Jakob Prandtauer. Through the gateway another similar but less elaborate central porch is visible. On each side of the window parts of obelisks can be seen, resting on a base which is as high as the columns of the porch. *See* 29, 75, 176, 184.

109: SPITTAL, CARINTHIA. A wrought iron gate in Castle Porcia; the castle 1539—1600, is a rare example of pure Italian Renaissance architecture in Austria. *See* 118, 152.

110: SALZBURG. Arcades in the courtyard of the former hospital, 1556—62, built very close to the steep rocks behind. The *Bürgerspital* was partially destroyed during the war and the parts that remain are now a dwelling house.

111: BRUCK, STYRIA. Arcades of the so called *Kornmesserhaus* 1499—1505, obviously inspired by Venetian examples and built in the flowery style of late Venetian Gothic.

112: EISENSTADT, BURGENLAND. Steps leading up from the little courtyard to the house in which Haydn lived from 1766—78. The house is now a museum dedicated to the memory of Haydn, Franz Liszt and the dancer Fanny Elssler.

113: STEYR, UPPER AUSTRIA. A late Gothic arcaded courtyard of a particularly picturesque house dating from 1520—5, the so-called *Stippelhof* now the Pharmacy of the Holy Ghost.

114: SALZBURG. Another view of the *Residenzbrunnen* which was erected 1656—61, possibly by Tommaso Garone. There are four horses round the rocks that form the base, on the top of which stands a group of nude men carrying a large flat basin with dolphins, which in their turn hold a smaller basin in which sits a Triton blowing water through a shell. This Triton and other motifs are reminiscent of Bernini's Roman fountains. *See* 104, 117, 159.

115: KREMSMÜNSTER, UPPER AUSTRIA. The five fishponds of the Benedictine Abbey, four of which were built 1690—2 by the Italian architect Carlo Antonio Carlone, the fifth was added by Jakob Prandtauer in 1715. *See* 140, 178.

116 and 117: SALZBURG. These colonnades erected in 1660 by G. A. Dario link the Archbishop's Palace (the *Residenz*) with the Cathedral and at the same time enhance the square in front of the Cathedral and make it into something of a precinct. On page 117 the Cathedral in seen on the left and in the foreground is one of Salzburg's many fountains the *Residenzbrunnen*. *See* 114, 159.

118: SPITTAL, CARINTHIA. The arcaded courtyard of Castle Porcia is pure Italian Renaissance architecture though perhaps a little overdecorated and not in quite the correct proportions. *See* 109.

119: ST. FLORIAN, UPPER AUSTRIA. In 1071 the Augustinian Canons took over an already existing monastery. The abbey and its church were completely rebuilt from 1686 onwards, first by C. A. Carlone and after his death in 1707 by Jakob Prandtauer, Austria's foremost architect of ecclesiastical Baroque buildings. The Marble Hall seen here from the principal staircase was built 1718—24. *See* 120, 121, 151, 153, 154, 155, 156, 183.

120 and 121: ST. FLORIAN, UPPER AUSTRIA. The left and central part of the principal staircase which is open to the quadrangle — an idea derived from Italy. The staircase was built by Prandtauer 1718—24. *See* 119, 151, 153, 154, 155, 156, 183.

122 and 123: ST. STEPHEN'S, VIENNA. The extraordinarily large traceried gables, each erected above a double window help to create a smooth transition from the wall to the enormous roof. The tracery of one of these gables dates from the mid fifteenth century when the nave was finished, the others were cut later in 1854. *See* 64, 65, 66, 134, 135, 166.

124: SCHÖNGRABERN, LOWER AUSTRIA. Above the window on the south side of the apse is shown the head of God the Father; flanked on one side by the dove of the Holy Ghost above the six jugs of Cana and on the other by the Virgin and Child. Below the window the Fall is depicted, Eve is shown seized by a demon and Adam by the devil. On the left of the window is the Last Judgement showing the dead man with the devil above him and St. Michael next to him. On the right is the Condemnation of Vanity or a Descent into Hell. The curious half columns are richly decorated and stand on consols carved as heads. *See* 216—19.

125: GURK, CARINTHIA. The three apses of the cathedral which was finished c. 1200. The masonry is particularly beautiful and the sparse decoration comprising shafts and blind arcades gives great dignity to the building. *See* 60, 142, 143, 158, 161, 172.

126: VIENNA. The equestrian statue of the Emperor Joseph II by A. Zauner was finished in 1806. The restrained mood of this sculpture matches its background, the National Library begun by J. B. Fischer von Erlach and finished by his son. The central part, seen here, was built 1723—6.

127: SALZBURG. This statue of the Immaculate Conception was designed by W. Hagenauer and the sculptures executed by J. Hagenauer 1766—71. Although this statue was created in the spirit of the Baroque it shows that this style was already on the wane. The sculptures are calmer and more composed than those on pages 106 and 107. The façade of the cathedral can be seen in the background.

128: SALZBURG. The group of the horsetamer from the *Hofstallschwemme* another of Salzburg's horse ponds, sculpted •1695 by M. B. Mandl.

129: VIENNA. Hercules and Medusa by H. Scherpe, a group of sculptures on the façade of the former imperial palace (the *Hofburg*). These sculptures as well as the façade date from the last decade of the nineteenth century. This part of the *Hofburg* although built so late was based on the designs of Fischer von Erlach.

130: INNSBRUCK, TYROL. Several sixteenth-century houses with variously shaped bay windows, some with late Gothic tracery, some with Renaissance decoration.

132: ZWETTL, LOWER AUSTRIA. The choir of the abbey church was built by Master Johannes between 1360 and 1383. The choir itself, the aisles and the ambulatory rise to the same height giving the impression of great spaciousness. *See* 133, 162, 163, 164, 165.

133: ZWETTL, LOWER AUSTRIA. A view into the right aisle of the choir towards the ambulatory. The vaults are simple quadripartite rib vaults. *See* 71, 132, 162, 163, 164, 165.

134: VIENNA. Figures of saints standing under high canopies, enrich the mighty piers of St. Stephen's. This part of the cathedral, its nave and aisles date from the fourteenth century.

135: VIENNA. The pulpit of St. Stephen's (by A. Pilgram, *c.* 1500) is an example of the very late ornate Gothic; the busts represent the Fathers of the Church. *See* 64, 65, 122, 123, 134, 166.

136: ST. VALENTIN, LOWER AUSTRIA. A view along the nave towards the west. The aisles are the same height as the nave and the rather flat, very decorative vaults. The columns separating the nave and aisles are very slender. This very late Gothic part of the church was finished in 1522.

137: SCHWAZ, TYROL. The parish church is a rare example of a church with four aisles; all the aisles are the same height; the ribs of the very complex Late Gothic vault spring directly and without interruption from the slender piers. The church built between the years 1489 and 1502, was rebuilt in the eighteenth century and extensively restored in 1909—10.

138: MARIA SAAL, CARINTHIA. The tomb of St. Modestus, a re-used late Roman sarcophagus under a Carolingian altar, stands in a special enclosure within the church. *See* 61, 139, 167, 179, 191, 192.

139: MARIA SAAL, CARINTHIA. The photograph shows the stairs to the gallery of the parish church and below them the font, an antique bowl with a cover that dates from 1711; next to the font is an ancient sarcophagus. *See* 61, 138, 167, 179, 191, 192.

140: KREMSMÜNSTER, UPPER AUSTRIA. The figure on the tomb dating from the fourteenth century represents the idealized image of the son of the founder of this Benedictine abbey, Duke Tassilo of Bavaria. The abbey was founded in his memory in 777. Parts of the fabric were restored in 1947. *See* 115, 178.

141: WIENER NEUSTADT, LOWER AUSTRIA. The photograph shows the west end of the parish church built in transitional style between the years 1259—1300. *See* 236, 242, 243.

142 and 143: GURK, CARINTHIA. The crypt of the cathedral was built 1160—74; one hundred white marble columns with block capitals support the curiously stilted groin vault. *See* 60, 125, 158, 161, 172.

144: LILIENFELD, LOWER AUSTRIA. The interior of the abbey church which was built in the early thirteenth century. *See* 32, 88.

145: ST. PAUL, CARINTHIA. A view of the interior of the church of the Benedictine abbey of St. Paul, begun after 1170 and restored in 1937. The arches and ribs show the strength of an early Romanesque church. The richly decorated block capital in the foreground is early Romanesque, the voluted capital in the background is slightly later. *See* 168, 169, 170.

146: HEILIGENKREUZ, LOWER AUSTRIA. A view of the cloisters of the Cistercian abbey which were built *c.* 1220—50. The capitals are characteristic of the transitional period between Romanesque and Gothic. *See* 147.

147: HEILIGENKREUZ, LOWER AUSTRIA. A Holy Water font at the entrance to the abbey church. *See* 146.

148: EISENSTADT, BURGENLAND. The mausoleum of Haydn, erected after 1930 in the *Bergkirche*.

149: LILIENFELD, LOWER AUSTRIA. The cloisters of the Cistercian abbey, *c.* 1250 built in very early Gothic. *See* 32, 144.

150: INNSBRUCK, TYROL. These arcades in the Herzog-Friedrich-Strasse are very characteristic of the oldest part of the city; most of them date from the sixteenth century.

151: ST. FLORIAN, UPPER AUSTRIA. These arcades were built by C. A. Carlone, the architect who began to rebuild the abbey in 1686. *See* 119, 120, 153, 154, 155, 183.

152: SPITTAL, CARINTHIA. The arcaded courtyard of Porcia Castle has the true flavour of the Italian Renaissance. *See* 109, 118.

153: ST. FLORIAN, UPPER AUSTRIA. Two columns with richly carved capitals and some cast iron decoration from the principal staircase of the abbey. *See* 119, 120, 121, 151, 154, 155, 183.

154: ST. FLORIAN, UPPER AUSTRIA. A view across the open staircase to the opposite wing of the abbey. *See* 119, 120, 121, 151, 153, 155, 183.

155: ST. FLORIAN, UPPER AUSTRIA. A view of the left arm of the staircase with richly decorated vaults which are characteristic of the Baroque of the first and second decade of the eighteenth century. *See* 119, 120, 121, 151, 153, 154, 156, 183.

156: ST. FLORIAN, UPPER AUSTRIA. Capitals, architrave and some of the ceiling frescoes of the abbey church, remodelled by Carlantonio Carlone 1696—1708; the decorations are by Bartholomeo Carlone, the frescoes by J.A.Gumpp and Melchior Steidl. *See* 119, 120, 121, 151, 153, 154, 155, 183.

# 6 LOOK UPWARDS!

158: GURK, CARINTHIA. The apse of the cathedral was built *c.* 1180. The sculpture represents a lion killing a dragon — a symbol of Christ vanquishing the forces of evil. *See* 60, 125, 142, 143, 161, 172.

159: SALZBURG. The Triton of the *Residenzbrunnen* 1656—61, perhaps by Tommaso Garone. *See* 104, 114, 117.

160: GRAZ, STYRIA. A view of the vault of the cathedral, built 1438—62 by the Emperor Friedrich III. The paintings of arms indicating the various imperial possessions were uncovered during restoration work in 1931.

161: GURK, CARINTHIA. A view of the late Gothic vault of the north aisle of the cathedral which was rebuilt after a fire in 1525. *See* 60, 125, 142, 143, 158, 172.

162: ZWETTL, LOWER AUSTRIA. A view into the vaults of the two western bays of the abbey church. These two bays were erected by Joseph Munggenast, the architect of the west façade, in the eighteenth century in imitation of the vaults of the Gothic part of the church. *See* 71, 132, 133, 163, 164, 165.

163: ZWETTL, LOWER AUSTRIA. A view of the vault in the ambulatory of the abbey church; the choir with the transept and the ambulatory was erected by Master Johannes of Vienna 1360—83; the chapels date from 1343—8. *See* 71, 132, 133, 162, 164, 169.

164 and 165: ZWETTL, LOWER AUSTRIA. Views of the windows and vault of the ambulatory surrounding the choir, built 1360—83 by Master Johannes of Vienna. *See* 71, 132, 133, 162, 163.

166: VIENNA. The organ loft of St. Stephen's seen from below. It was built in very late Gothic style by Master Anton Pilgram, who represented himself carrying the vault, 1512—13. *See* 64, 65, 66, 122, 123, 134, 135.

167: MARIA SAAL, CARINTHIA. The West gallery belongs to the mid fifteenth century, when the church was first built; the balustrade was replaced in 1734 by a richly carved late Baroque parapet and the organ. *See* 61, 138, 139, 179, 191, 192.

168: ST. PAUL, CARINTHIA. A crucifix, seen from below, against the vault of the Romanesque abbey church. *See* 145, 169, 170.

169: ST. PAUL, CARINTHIA. The sounding board of the late Baroque pulpit, seen against the ribs and the arches of the Romanesque abbey church. *See* 145, 168, 170.

170: ST. PAUL, CARINTHIA. Richly carved capitals dating from the early thirteenth century in the twelfth-century church. *See* 145, 158, 169.

171: GÖSS, STYRIA. Church of the former Benedictine convent, 1510—21, with very complex late Gothic rib vaults which have no constructional purpose and are purely decorative.

172: GURK, CARINTHIA. A Romanesque capital in the cathedral decorated with vine leaves and heads which dates from about 1190. The bishop's staff which can be seen in front of it belongs to a figure on the high altar built between 1629 and 1632. *See* 60, 125, 142, 143, 158, 161.

173: MILLSTATT, CARINTHIA. Parts of the jambs and voussoir of the church of the former Benedictine abbey which dates from the twelfth century. The decorations are rich and show a great variety of Romanesque patterns.

174: BRAUNAU, UPPER AUSTRIA. The processional pole of the Stonemason's Guild seen against the late Gothic vaults of the parish church. *See* 69.

175: INNSBRUCK, TYROL. Arcades in the Herzog-Friedrich-Strasse with late Gothic vaulting dating from the sixteenth century.

176: MELK, LOWER AUSTRIA. The staircase leading into one of the towers of the abbey church. *See* 29, 75, 108, 184.

177: SALZBURG. View through the vault from one of the chapels of the University Church upwards to the roof of the gallery. The stucco is probably the work of Francesco Carlone and Paolo de Allio and their assistants. *See* 100.

178: KREMSMÜNSTER, UPPER AUSTRIA. The church of the Benedictine abbey, originally built in Romanesque and Gothic was remodelled in the Baroque style in 1680. The decorations by G. B. Colombo, G. B. Barbarino and their assistants follow the medieval vaulting system and though very rich they do not show the same exuberance as later Baroque decoration. *See* 115, 140.

179: MARIA SAAL, CARINTHIA. The late Gothic vault dates from the fifteenth century. On it a representation of the Tree of Jesse is painted; the figures grow out of flowers, and in between them are decorative motifs. *See* 61, 138, 139, 167, 191, 192.

180: HERZOGENBURG, LOWER AUSTRIA. The abbey church built 1743—50 perhaps by Joseph Munggenast was fitted in 1780 with an ornate organ, where Baroque ornaments mingle with Rococo motifs.

181: SCHWAZ, TYROL. View towards the west gallery of the parish church; this was added 1518—22 by Konrad Vogel of Frankfurt. The organ was built in 1730 by a local man, Bartholomäus Alter.

182: STAMS, TYROL. This elaborate wrought iron gate by B. Bachnetzer dating from 1716 separates the Chapel of the Holy Blood from the narthex of the church of the Cistercian abbey.

183: ST. FLORIAN, UPPER AUSTRIA. View into the nave of the abbey church. The stucco decorations are by Bartholomeo Carlone, the frescoes by J. A. Gumpp and Melchior Steidl and the wrought iron gate (1698) by Hans Messner from Passau. *See* 119, 120, 121, 151, 153, 154, 155, 156.

184: MELK, LOWER AUSTRIA. View into the dome of the abbey church, erected 1712—14; J. M. Rottmayr painted the figures, and Gaetano Fanti the architectural details of the fresco in the dome; the highly elaborate design was devised by Abbot Dietmayr. *See* 29, 75, 108, 176, 184.

185: SALZBURG. Church of St. Erhard, Nonntal near Salzburg; the figure of St. Rupertus with two angels and a model of the church is fitted into a spandrel carrying the dome. The church was built 1685—9 by Caspar Zugalli, the sculptures are by Francesco Brenno.

186: ALTENBURG, LOWER AUSTRIA. A detail from the church of the Benedictine abbey which was remodelled in the Baroque style in 1730—3 by Munggenast.

187: WILHERING, UPPER AUSTRIA. The church of the Cistercian abbey was rebuilt in 1733, possibly after a design by Andrea Altomonte. It is a rare example of Rococo in Austria; some characteristic Rococo motifs can be seen behind the two *putti* who are shown playing lightheartedly.

188: VORAU, STYRIA. God the Father and angels in an aureole — a detail from the High Baroque decoration of the first third of the eighteenth century. The church, the abbey church of the Augustinian Canons, is now also the parish church; it was rebuilt 1660—2 in the style of Carlone. *See* 208, 209.

190: ST. MAREIN NEAR KNITTELFELD, STYRIA. A late Gothic altar-piece donated by Abbot G. Schärdinger in 1524, representing the Virgin and Child with two saints, formerly in the Church of St. Martha, now in the parish church.

191: MARIA SAAL, CARINTHIA. A late Gothic altar-piece of *c.* 1520; the Virgin with the Christ child and St. Anne on her arms, accompanied by two female saints on each side. The altar-piece now in the parish church of Maria Saal was made for the church of Arndorf. *See* 61, 138, 139, 167, 179, 192.

192: MARIA SAAL, CARINTHIA. A coronation of the Virgin — Christ and God the Father are holding the crown over the kneeling Virgin; a detail of the late Gothic altar-piece (*c.* 1520) now in the parish church of Maria Saal. *See* 61, 138, 139, 167, 179, 191.

193: GRIES NEAR BOLZANO, SOUTH TYROL. This carving, the Coronation of the Virgin, is all that has survived from the altar-piece in the parish church; it is an early work by Michael Pacher, commissioned between 1471 and 1475. Mary is represented kneeling, with Christ and God the Father, one on each side, blessing her. The frame is enriched by angels playing musical instruments.

194: MONDSEE, UPPER AUSTRIA. *Putti* supporting columns, carved by Meinrad Guggenbichler 1682—4, which are copies of those early Christian columns still surviving in St. Peter's, Rome, that, according to tradition, came from the Temple of Solomon. *See* 204, 232, 246, 249.

195: ST. WOLFGANG, UPPER AUSTRIA. The figure of St. Wolfgang holding a model of the church, from the great altar-piece of the parish church. This, Michael Pacher's masterpiece (1471—86), is outstanding among Gothic altar-pieces. *See* 202, 203, 206, 207, 223, 248, 251.

196: MARIA GAIL, CARINTHIA. A panel with the Nativity from a late Gothic altar-piece in the parish church. *See* 197.

197: MARIA GAIL, CARINTHIA. Another panel from the same altar-piece showing the Adoration of the Magi. *See* 196.

198 and 199: INNSBRUCK, TYROL. The Mausoleum of Emperor Maximilian I in the *Hofkirche;* the Emperor is kneeling on the sarcophagus, designed by Alexander and

Abraham Colin; the four corner figures represent four virtues, and were designed by Alexander Colin. On each side of the sarcophagus are figures representing the Emperor's ancestors; three of these figures were designed by Dürer. The Mausoleum was originally planned on an even grander scale; the work was started at the beginning of the sixteenth century and was not completed in its present form until after 1580.

200: LIEDING, CARINTHIA. The late Baroque High Altar (dating from 1770) in the parish church was carved by Georg Hittinger; the Virgin and Child appear under a canopy in an aureole studded with angels' heads; other angels hold back a curtain. God the Father, also in an aureole, gives his blessing. The whole effect is one of incredible grace and lightness.

201: CHRISTKINDL, UPPER AUSTRIA. The Holy Ghost is depicted as a dove in an aureole surrounded by clouds and dancing angels, God the Father hovers above; the whole work is precariously balanced on the top of the High Altar, which was designed c. 1710, possibly by Jakob Prandtauer.

202 and 203: ST. WOLFGANG, UPPER AUSTRIA. Details from the Altar of the Rosary — the sculptures (1706)

are by Meinrad Guggenbichler; statues of Abraham and Isaac (page 202) and of the Archangel Raphael with Tobias (page 203) stand one on each side of the painted altar-piece. *See* 195, 206, 207, 223, 248, 251.

204: MONDSEE, UPPER AUSTRIA. The statue of St. Rochus, carved c. 1685 by Meinrad Guggenbichler, formerly belonged to an altar but now forms part of a tomb in the parish church. *See* 194, 202—3, 232, 246, 249.

205: ST. GEORGEN AN DER MATTIG, UPPER AUSTRIA. St. Martin and the Beggar, the centre part of an altar-piece. The St. Martin's Altar is one of three created by Martin and Michael Zürn c. 1645—50.

206 and 207: ST. WOLFGANG, UPPER AUSTRIA. St. Christopher (page 206) and figures from the Holy Family (page 207) — both details from the large double altar-piece in the parish church, were carved by Thomas Schwanthaler. *See* 195, 202, 203, 248, 251.

208 and 209: VORAU, STYRIA. The angels and angels' heads are from the High Baroque decorations of the parish church. The church was rebuilt 1660—2 and decorated between 1700 and 1730. *See* 188.

# 7 CARVING

210: SALZBURG. A detail from the balustrade of the grand staircase of Mirabell Castle, which was rebuilt 1721—7 by Lukas von Hildebrand, the contemporary of Fischer von Erlach, Austria's other great Baroque architect. The *putto* balancing on the scroll was, like other similar ones, carved in the *atelier* of Raphael Donner.

211: OBERHOFEN, UPPER AUSTRIA. Angels balancing on clouds — detail from an altar of the parish church. Dating from 1712, it is a late work by Meinrad Guggenbichler.

212: JUDENBURG, STYRIA. A statue of the Virgin and Child, a so-called *Schöne Madonna*, from the Chapel

of Our Lady in the parish church, carved c. 1420 by Master Hans of Judenburg. The arrangement of the drapery and the posture of the Virgin is typical of the early fifteenth century.

213: GRAZ, STYRIA. The Madonna and Child from the tympanum of the west portal of the *Leechkirche* is a masterpiece of Austrian early Gothic sculpture; the group dates from the last quarter of the thirteenth century. The Virgin is represented enthroned and crowned, holding a pomegranate; her feet rest on two dragons. *See* 103.

214: IRRSDORF, SALZBURG. The reliefs on the doors of the Gothic church represent Mary and Elizabeth; they date from c. 1408.

216: SCHÖNGRABERN, LOWER AUSTRIA. Detail of the sculptural decorations from the apse of the parish church which date from the first third of the thirteenth century. This scene represents the Fall, Eve has been seized by a demon and Adam by the devil. *See* 124, 217, 218, 219.

217: SCHÖNGRABERN, LOWER AUSTRIA. Detail of the sculptural decoration of the apse. A man who is holding a dog on a leash is about to hit a lion with an axe; another dog attacks the beast from behind. *See* 124, 216, 218, 219.

218: SCHÖNGRABERN, LOWER AUSTRIA. Detail from the sculptures of the apse. A bear has seized a man who is trying to stick his knife into him; a huntsman rushing in attacks the bear with a lance. The figure behind the bear is probably a dog attacking it, but may be a bear cub hiding. This scene is above one of a fight with the lion; although these scenes appear to have no relationship with the holy story it must be assumed that they are symbolic probably of the fight of man against evil. *See* 124, 216, 217, 219.

219: SCHÖNGRABERN, LOWER AUSTRIA. Details from the sculptures of the apse showing Christ enthroned, and below him a dragon who is about to swallow a man while holding another in his claws. The lamb on the left belongs to Adam bringing a sacrifice; he is partnered by Cain with a sheaf of corn (not on the photograph). *See* 124, 216–18.

220: ST. VEIT, CARINTHIA. The head of the Christ from a crucifixion dating from *c.* 1500. The agony of pain is expressed in the very naturalistic manner of late Gothic sculpture. *See* 225.

221: MARIA STRASSENGEL, STYRIA. This Lamentation over the body of Christ comes from the tympanum of the south porch and dates from the second half of the fourteenth century. *See* 68.

222: MAUER NEAR MELK, LOWER AUSTRIA. Heads and hands of figures from the lower panel of the altarpiece of the parish church of c. 1513–16. *See* 226–31, 256.

223: ST. WOLFGANG, UPPER AUSTRIA. The Hand of the Lord, blessing — a detail from Pacher's altar-piece in the parish church, 1471–81. *See* 195, 202, 203, 206, 207, 248, 251.

224: SALZBURG. Part of a Crucifix, now in Nonnberg Monastery, early fourteenth century. *See* 245.

225: ST. VEIT, CARINTHIA. Another detail from a crucifixion seen in the parish church, *c.* 1500. *See* 220.

226 and 227: MAUER NEAR MELK, LOWER AUSTRIA. Detail from the lower half of the altar-piece in the parish church—saints looking up to the Coronation of the Virgin, *c.* 1520. *See* 222, 228, 229, 230, 231, 256.

228: MAUER NEAR MELK, LOWER AUSTRIA. A statue of the Virgin and Child held up by angels, a detail from the upper part of the altar. Other angels (not on the photograph) hold the crown over the Virgin's head. This is a very unusual representation of the Coronation of the Virgin, *c.* 1520. *See* 222, 226, 227, 229–31, 256.

228: MAUER NEAR MELK, LOWER AUSTRIA. A group of angels, some dressed, some nude, playing the flute. From the altar-piece in the parish church, *c.* 1520. *See* 222, 226, 227, 228, 230, 231, 256.

230 and 231: MAUER NEAR MELK, LOWER AUSTRIA. Other groups of angels from the altar-piece in the parish church, *c.* 1520. *See* 222, 226–29, 256.

232: MONDSEE, UPPER AUSTRIA. Heads of two angels by Meinrad Guggenbichler from one of the altar-pieces in the parish church, 1684. *See* 194, 204, 246, 249.

233: IRRSDORF, SALZBURG. An angel from an altar-piece by Meinrad Guggenbichler in the Church of the Virgin, 1684. *See* 235, 247, 256.

234: SEEKIRCHEN, SALZBURG. A statue of the Madonna and Child in the abbey church dating from the eighteenth century; this sculpture has been attributed to various masters, including Simeon Friess and Meinrad Guggenbichler.

235: IRRSDORF, SALZBURG. Another angel from an altar-piece by Meinrad Guggenbichler in the church of the Holy Virgin, 1684. *See* 233, 247, 256.

236: WIENER NEUSTADT, LOWER AUSTRIA. The Apostle Thomas; one of twelve statues of the apostles attached to the piers of the cathedral in the same way as similar figures in Stephen's, Vienna. The figures were carved by Lorenz Luchsberger at the end of the fifteenth century. *See* 141, 242, 243.

237: INZERSDORF, UPPER AUSTRIA. The head of a statue of the Virgin, *c.* 1420–30, another *Schöne Madonna*, *See* 212.

238 and 239: IMST, TYROL. Masks used in the *Schemenlaufen* of Imst, a festival of great interest to students of folklore and one of pagan persuasion, in which pagan rites of exorcism are imitated.

240 and 241: VIENNA. Two busts by F. X. Messerschmidt, made between *c.* 1770 and the sculptor's death in 1783, now in the Baroque Museum, Belvedere: page 240 shows "The Ill-humoured One" *(Der Griesgrämige)* and page 241 "The Fool" *(Der Schalksnarr).* It is now known that these heads are not expressions of mood or character, but that they are evidence of the sculptor's disordered mind.

242 and 243: WIENER NEUSTADT, LOWER AUSTRIA. Heads of the apostles Peter and Philip from statues on the nave piers of the cathedral dating from the end of the fifteenth century. *See* 141, 236.

244: KEFERMARKT, UPPER AUSTRIA. The head of St. Christopher is the most remarkable figure of an outstanding altar-piece and one of the masterpieces of late Gothic carving. It was created by an unknown sculptor between 1490 and 1498. *See* 254.

245: SALZBURG. The head of Christ from the Crucifixion in Nonnberg Convent; first half of the fourteenth century. *See* 224.

246: MONDSEE, UPPER AUSTRIA. The head of St. Benedict, by Meinrad Guggenbichler, from the Altar of the Holy Ghost in the parish church. It dates from 1679—81. *See* 194, 204, 232, 249.

247: IRRSDORF, SALZBURG. The head of St. Martin from the High Altar of the church. Also the work of Meinrad Guggenbichler it dates from 1682—4. *See* 233, 256.

248: ST. WOLFGANG, UPPER AUSTRIA. The head of St. Benedict from the altar-piece by Michael Pacher. It dates from 1471—81. *See* 195, 202, 203, 206, 207, 223, 251.

249: MONDSEE, UPPER AUSTRIA. Head of a Benedictine saint (St. Maurus or St. Placidus) from the Wolfgang Altar by Meinrad Guggenbichler, dating from 1679—81. *See* 194, 204, 232, 246.

250: HALLSTATT, UPPER AUSTRIA. A head of St. John from a Crucifixion group of *c.* 1510 in the Roman Catholic parish church. *See* 38.

251: ST. WOLFGANG, UPPER AUSTRIA. The head of the Virgin from the altar-piece by Michael Pacher, dating from 1471—81. *See* 195, 202, 203, 206, 207, 223, 248, 251.

252: PÖGGSTALL, LOWER AUSTRIA. Head of the Virgin, a statue in the parish church dating from the end of the fifteenth century.

253: SALZBURG. The head of the Virgin — the only statue that has survived from the Gothic altar-piece of the Franciscan church. This altar-piece was commissioned from Michael Pacher in 1484.

254: KEFERMARKT, UPPER AUSTRIA. St. Christopher carrying the Christ-child. A detail from the altar-piece in the parish church, 1490—8. *See* 244.

255: IRRSDORF, SALZBURG. The head of St. Virgil from the High Altar of the church by Meinrad Guggenbichler. It dates from 1682—4. *See* 233, 247.

256: MAUER, LOWER AUSTRIA. The bearded head of a statue of God the Father from the altar-piece in the parish church, *c.* 1520. *See* 222, 226, 227, 228, 229, 230, 231.

272